A GRANDFATHER'S MEMORY JOURNAL

Look back · Record · Treasure forever

Hardie Grant

QUADRILLE

THIS GRANDFATHER'S MEMORY
JOURNAL IS A GIFT TO

_____

WITH LOVE FROM

_____

Given name at birth

Date of birth

Place of birth

Relationship / marriage

Children

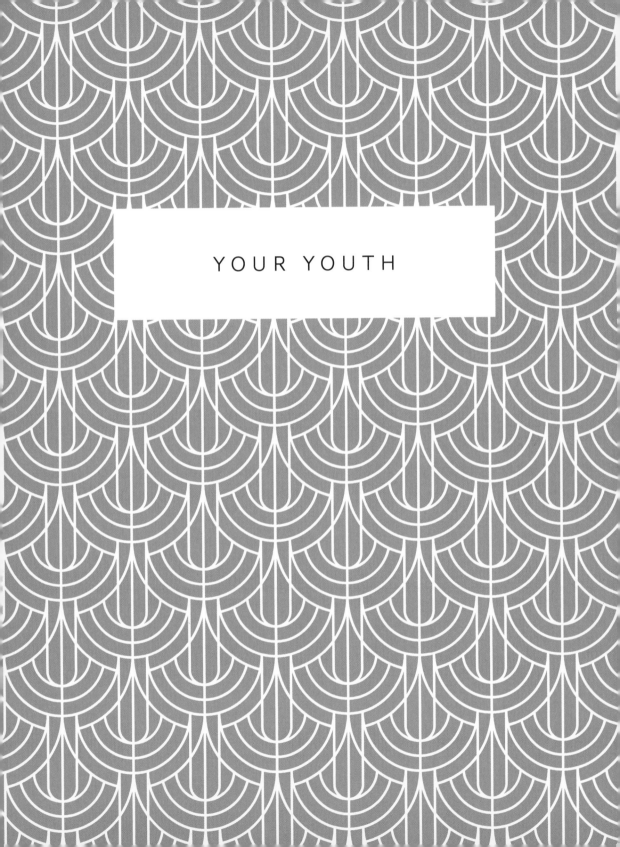

YOUR YOUTH

Your grandparents' names

Your grandparents' dates of birth

Where were your grandparents born?

What were your grandparents' occupations?

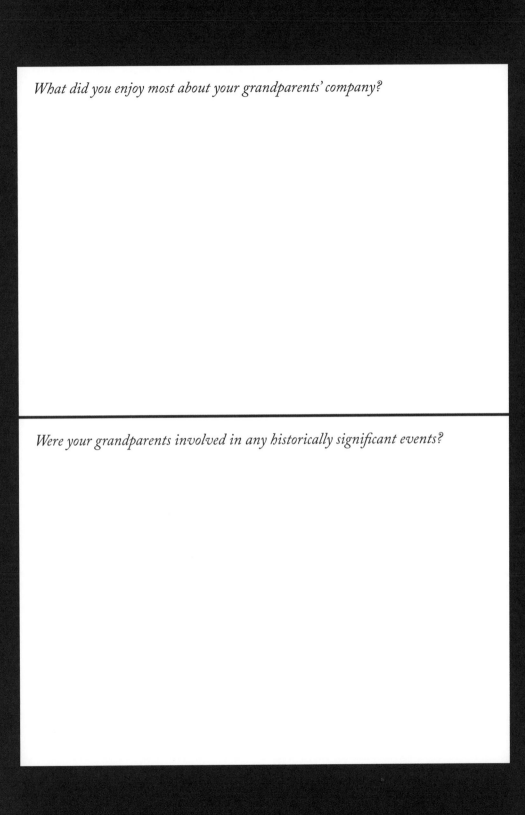

What did you enjoy most about your grandparents' company?

Were your grandparents involved in any historically significant events?

Have you inherited any family heirlooms?

Do you, or I, resemble any of our ancestors?

Your mother's name

Your mother's date of birth

Your mother's place of birth

Your mother's occupation

Your father's name

Your father's date of birth

Your father's place of birth

Your father's occupation

How did your parents meet?

What's your earliest memory of your mother and father?

Did your parents have a happy marriage?

What did you admire about your parents?

Can you describe your relationship with your parents?

*Have you discovered anything about your parents
that you didn't know when you were growing up?*

What's the most valuable lesson you learned from your parents?

Did you or your family experience any tragedies when you were growing up?

Who were the members of your immediate family?

What were the names of your siblings?

Where was your first family home?

Did you have any family pets?

Do you remember having a happy childhood?

What did you consider to be a real luxury as a child?

What were your favourite meals?

What was your most precious toy?

What outside games did you play?

When you were young, did you collect anything?

Did you face any real hardship when growing up?

Is there anything about your childhood that shocks you now?

What was the first piece of news you remember hearing as a child?

Which invention made a big impact on your childhood?

What work around the house / garden did you have to do?

Did your father or mother teach you any useful practical skills?

How religious were your family?

What were the highlights of the year for you as a child?

Which national events do you recall celebrating?

Did you have any childhood heroes?

Where did you go to school?

Which subjects did you enjoy at school?

Who were your closest friends at school?

Did you experience or witness harsh discipline at school?

Which playground games did you enjoy?

What qualifications did you achieve?

Were there any youthful fads you remember?

Were you a member of any clubs or societies?

Which forms of transport did you rely on when you were growing up?

What sports did you participate in?

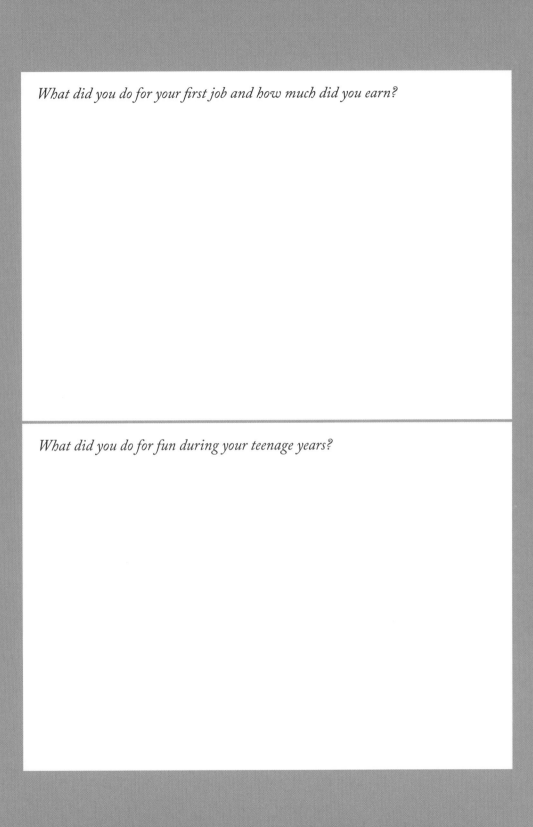

What did you do for your first job and how much did you earn?

What did you do for fun during your teenage years?

Who was your first crush?

Were you interested in popular music? If so, who did you listen to?

Did you enjoy reading?

What do you believe makes for a happy child?

What piece of advice would you pass to your 16-year-old self?

How has the area in which you grew up changed?

Is there anything from your childhood you miss?

Is there anyone from your childhood you miss?

ON BECOMING
AN ADULT

When did you leave home?

How much did your first house or flat cost to rent or buy?

Where was the first place you lived?

When did you first feel financially independent of your parents?

What's the first big purchase you remember making?

What was your first car or bike?

What is your favourite book / film / song?

Do you follow any sports teams?

What was the most enjoyable live sporting event / concert / play you've seen?

Which political parties / organisations / charities have you supported?

When were you the most physically fit?

Describe the most dramatic episode of your life

Have you made a serious mistake in your life?

Who has been the single most important person of your life?

Record your places of work and your position there

How important was your job to you?

FAM

TR

A family tree is a diagram which charts the relationships of each generation within a family. The branches of the tree connect each person to their parents, spouses and children.

You can start with the oldest generation at the top and the newer generations at the bottom. You can make it more complete by adding branches for cousins, aunts and uncles, or keep it focused and create a family tree with only parents, grandparents and siblings – it can be as simple or as complex as you like. For extra detail, you can record both maiden and married names, as well as dates of births and deaths.

MILY

EE

Describe a time when you felt most successful at work

Where did you most enjoy working?

When did you feel that your life was most useful?

When did you feel that your life was at its toughest?

What's the most brilliant thing that has ever happened to you?

Where's the most beautiful place you have visited?

Who's the most famous person you've met?

What skills have you learned in adult life?

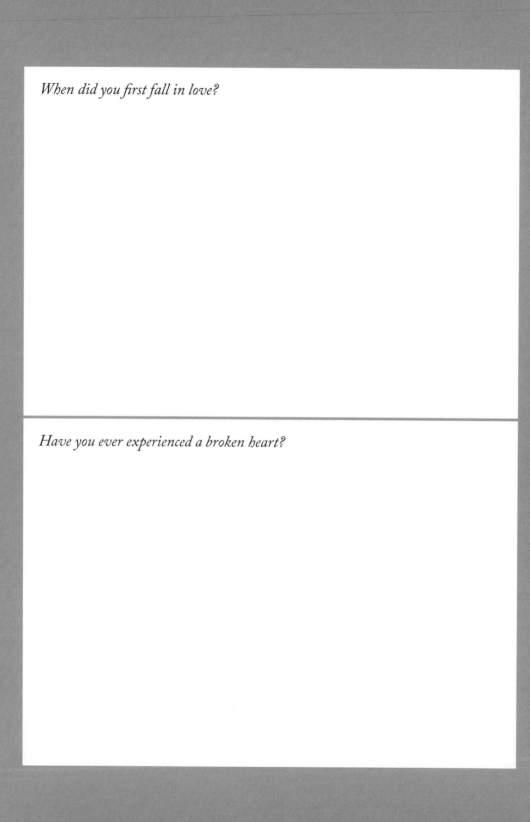

When did you first fall in love?

Have you ever experienced a broken heart?

How did you meet my grandmother?

When did you know you had fallen in love?

Did you have a stag night before you married? If so, what happened?

Record some of the highlights of your wedding day

What do you believe are the crucial ingredients for a good relationship?

Is there a particular place that reminds you of happy times with my grandmother?

ON BECOMING
A FATHER

Names of your children

Dates of birth of your children

Where were they born?

Did you have any children that are no longer here?

What can you remember about the birth of my mother / father?

What was family life like with your children and my grandmother?

What did you enjoy about the baby years?

How involved did you get with nappies and bedtimes?

Can you remember my mother / father's first words?

What activities did you like to share with my mother / father?

What did you think it was important to teach my mother / father?

Did you find any aspects of being a parent stressful?

Were you a strict father?

Where did you go on holiday as a young family?

Recall a special time spent with my mother / father

Record a funny incident you remember about my mother / father as a child

Did my mother / father have a particular expression
or habit that you remember fondly?

What did my mother / father do to make you proud?

Were you an affectionate family?

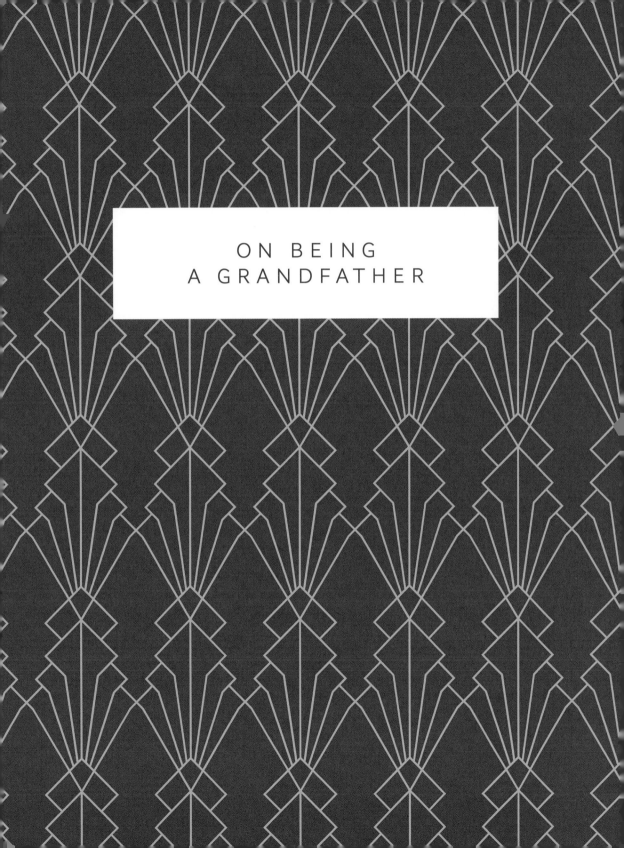

ON BEING
A GRANDFATHER

Names of your grandchildren

Can you describe how you felt when I was born?

Had you an idea in mind as to the sort of grandfather you wanted to be?

How does being a grandfather compare to being a father?

Which aspect of being a grandfather has given you the most pleasure?

What similarities do I share with you?

Describe me in a few words

Describe a special memory of time spent with me

What are your hopes for me as I grow older?

What would your hopes be for my grandchildren?

How different are you to your grandfather?

What would I be surprised to discover about you?

What's the most valuable lesson you've learned from me?

Is there something you enjoyed doing as a child that you could show / teach me?

What fun shall we have together in the future?

CHANGING TIMES

What do you think has been the greatest invention in your lifetime?

Which global or national events have had the most impact on your life?

Do you remember your reaction to key historic events
(such as the fall of the Berlin Wall or 9/11)?

Have your political affiliations changed over your lifetime?

Has your outlook on life changed over your lifetime?

Are there any family war stories you would like to record?

Are there lessons from history you think we should learn?

Have attitudes to men changed during your lifetime?

What has been the greatest social change for the better in your lifetime?

Are there any figures – historical or personal – that you admire?

Has the world improved since you were born?

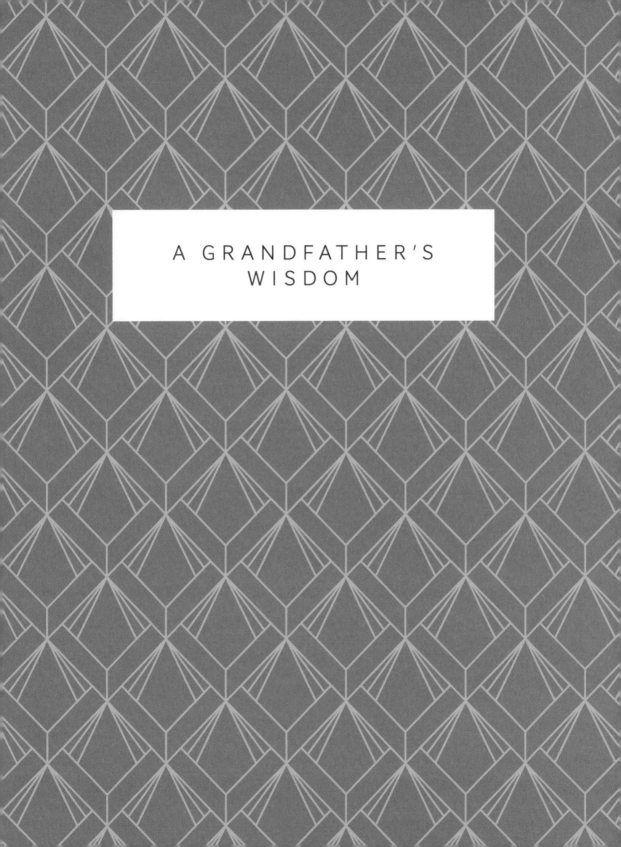

A GRANDFATHER'S WISDOM

What's the key to happiness?

What has been your favourite stage of life?

What's the hardest choice you've ever had to make?

What's the best decision you've ever made?

Do you have any, as yet, unrealised dreams?

What are you thankful for?

What is your philosophy of life?

Describe a piece of news / book / painting / film
that made a big impact on how you think

Whether in your personal or working life, when have you achieved something that's really helped other people?

What's your advice for overcoming hard times or adversity?

Is there a quote that is particularly meaningful to you?

How would you like to be remembered?

What's the most useful piece of advice you've been given and who shared it with you?

If you could pass on only one piece of advice, what would it be?

What are the three most important elements of a happy family?

Are there any family traditions you would like me to continue?

BUSINESS DEVELOPMENT DIRECTOR Melanie Gray

ASSISTANT EDITOR Stacey Cleworth

AUTHOR Joanna Gray

DESIGNERS Katherine Keeble and Gemma Hayden

PRODUCTION DIRECTOR Vincent Smith

PRODUCTION CONTROLLER Sinead Hering

Published in 2019 by Quadrille,
an imprint of Hardie Grant Publishing

Quadrille
52–54 Southwark Street
London SE1 1UN
quadrille.com

ISBN 978 1 78713 497 3

Printed in China